# When the Chains Fall off

by

# Thuli Marutle Leigh

WHEN THE CHAINS FALL OFF
Reclaiming Dreams, Dignity & Equality in Marriage and Relationships
© 2025 Thuli Marutle Leigh
All rights reserved.

No part of this book may be reproduced, distributed, or transmitted in any form or by any means, including photocopying, recording, or other electronic or mechanical methods, without prior written permission from the author.

This is a work of nonfiction. Some names and identifying details have been changed to protect privacy. Any resemblance to actual persons or situations is coincidental.

Author: Thuli Marutle Leigh
Email: mt.marutle@gmail.com

Unauthorized distribution is strictly prohibited.

# Dedication

For every woman who was told her place was only in the home — may you remember the little girl who once dreamed boldly before you met him. May you find your voice again, demand respect, dream fearlessly, and rise.
And to every man who has ever feared a strong woman — may you learn that partnership builds empires, while control builds cages that eventually break love.

# Preface

This book is for the woman who finally realized she was losing herself in the name of love, loyalty, and endurance. For the woman who poured until she was empty, who stayed quiet to keep the peace, and who forgot that she, too, deserved the life she once dreamed of.

It is not a story of rebellion, but of awakening. Not revenge, but restoration.

This is about choosing yourself — your voice, your dignity, your joy — even when it feels uncomfortable, unfamiliar, or frightening. It is the moment a woman remembers her worth and walks toward the light again, leaving behind the chains that once held her down.

May these pages remind you that choosing yourself is not selfish.
It is survival.
It is strength.
It is freedom.

# TABLE OF CONTENTS

PART ONE — THE FAIRYTALE START

Chapter 1: The Charming Protector
Chapter 2: Leaving the World Behind
Chapter 3: The Golden Beginning

PART TWO — THE GOLDEN CAGE

Chapter 4: Motherhood & Isolation
Chapter 5: The Critic Emerges

PART THREE — COLLAPSE & AWAKENING

Chapter 6: The Weight of His Words
Chapter 7: Control & Dependence
Chapter 8: Cracks in the Throne

PART FOUR — HER RISE & NEW POWER

Chapter 9: Picking Up the Pieces
Chapter 10: Finding Her Voice
Chapter 11: Rebuilding on Equality

EPILOGUE — Her New Beginning

About the Author

# Chapter 1: The Charming Protector

Before everything changed — before the chaos, the heartbreak, the awakening — there was Koketso.

Koketso was the kind of woman who carried her life with quiet dignity. Not loud, not flashy, not the type to compete for attention. There was a softness in the way she moved, the kind of gentleness that drew people in without her even trying. She wasn't the most glamorous woman, but she had something far more valuable — a warm spirit, the type that makes strangers open up to her without knowing why.

She was young, in her early 20s, working at a retail store in town.
A job some people might have looked down on — but Koketso loved it.

She loved talking to customers, arranging shelves, learning about products, even the small thrill of hitting daily targets. It wasn't her final destination, but it paid the bills, and more importantly, it kept her moving toward the future she imagined.

She had dreams.
Big ones.

From a young age, she wanted to become a psychologist — the person people go to when their hearts are heavy and their minds overwhelmed. She had always believed she had a calling to understand people deeply, to help them heal. And she was saving, little by little, to go to university. It would take time, but she was determined.

And then there was Tebogo.

Her boyfriend — the kind of man people don't appreciate until they lose.
He wasn't rich.
He wasn't polished.
He worked odd jobs — fixing things, delivering goods, helping small businesses — anything that paid. But what he lacked in money, he made up for in courage and effort.

Tebogo was a man with potential.

Hard-working.
Sweet.
Respectful.

Supportive.
Loyal.
Not perfect, but a good man with a good heart.

They dreamed together.
They planned together.
They were in love — deeply — but life was not easy for them.

There were nights they shared bread and tea because money was tight.
Days they walked long distances because taxis were a luxury.
Moments they held hands and encouraged each other not to give up.

Koketso had no intention of leaving Tebogo.
No matter how hard things were, she believed they were building something real.
They were going to rise together — slowly, maybe, but together.

And then one ordinary afternoon, life shifted.

She was standing behind the counter, scanning items, doing what she always did — greeting customers with her gentle smile — when Sipho walked in.

From the moment he stepped through the door, he felt… different.

Not necessarily better.
Just different.

He moved like a man who owned the air around him — confident, relaxed, smiling as if the world had never disappointed him. He wore cologne that announced his presence before he even spoke. His clothes were clean, sharp, expensive-looking without being loud.

Sipho didn't walk in to buy necessities.
He shopped like someone who came to release stress — picking things casually, throwing items into his basket without checking the price, treating the store as his playground.

People noticed.
Even Koketso did.

Not because she was impressed — but because such customers were rare.

When he reached her till, he greeted her with a charm so natural it almost felt scripted.

"How are you today, beautiful?"
His voice was smooth, warm, confident — but not arrogant.

Koketso gave the polite smile she gave all customers, but something about this man made her more aware of herself. She scanned his items, told him the price, packaged his things — keeping things professional.

Sipho watched her.
Not in a creepy way — in a way that made it clear he saw her.

"You have a lovely smile," he said casually, as if complimenting her was the most normal thing in the world.

She thanked him politely, ready for him to leave.

But he didn't.

He paused, leaning slightly closer — respectful, but intentional.

"Do you have WhatsApp?"

She froze for a second.

Customers flirted sometimes. Men asked for her number all the time. She always refused. She had a boyfriend she respected — and besides, she wasn't interested.

But Sipho wasn't like the others.
He wasn't begging.
He wasn't forcing.
He was simply... calm. Sure of himself.

"I just want to talk," he said, with a small smile. "Nothing more."

Something in his tone felt safe.
Or charming.
Or dangerous.
She couldn't tell.

Against her better judgment, Koketso hesitated — for just a second.

And Sipho knew that hesitation was an opening.

In that moment, her entire life was about to shift — not because she planned it, not because she was unhappy, not because she wanted someone new — but because life sometimes tests women with the one thing they think they can handle: attention.

She told herself:
It's just my number. It's harmless. I love Tebogo. Nothing will happen.

And so she gave it to him.

What started as "innocent talking" quickly turned into something else.

Sipho texted her good morning before Tebogo even woke up.
He sent her lunch money "so you don't eat snacks only."
He passed by the store just to see her smile.
He listened to her dreams like they were sacred.
He spoiled her — small things at first, then bigger things.
He pursued her like a man who knew what he wanted and wasn't afraid to claim it.

He made her feel like the world had finally placed her at the center.

And slowly — so slowly she didn't even notice — the love she had for Tebogo began to dim.
Not because he did anything wrong.
But because she gave Sipho time…

And attention is fertilizer.
It grows whatever you water.

This was only the beginning.

What Koketso didn't know was that Sipho could see something in her — something she didn't even see in herself yet.

A softness ready to be molded.
A heart ready to be convinced.
A dreamer who just needed the right push… or the right trap.

And that is how a chapter that looks harmless in the beginning
becomes the reason a woman's whole life takes a different turn.

# Chapter 2: Leaving the World Behind

For weeks after giving Sipho her number, Koketso told herself nothing serious would happen. She convinced herself she was just being friendly, that she wasn't doing anything wrong. After all, people talk to new people all the time... right?

But she felt it — the shift.

It started quietly.

Sipho's good morning texts arrived before Tebogo even sent his first one.
His "Did you eat?" messages came during her lunch break.
His compliments came when she wasn't expecting them.
His presence slowly filled the spaces of her day without her giving him permission.

Tebogo noticed the change long before he admitted it.

Koketso didn't stop loving him — but something in her was drifting.

A small seed of doubt.
A small whisper of comparison.
A small taste of something she had never experienced before.

Sipho showed her a different world, a faster world, a world where success wasn't a dream — it was already happening.
He had money.
He had stability.
He had direction.
He had confidence.
He had the kind of life Koketso believed she could build toward one day… but Sipho already lived in it.

It was intoxicating.

She found herself texting him back faster than she responded to Tebogo.
Laughing at Sipho's jokes harder than she meant to.
Checking her phone for Sipho's message before she even thought about Tebogo's.

It wasn't intentional.
It wasn't planned.
It just happened — quietly, softly, slowly.

That's how hearts shift.

Sipho made her feel seen in a way she didn't even know she was missing.
He made her feel chosen in ways that felt new and exciting.
He spoiled her with small things — takeaways on days she was tired, taxi money when he knew she walked too much, little gifts he dropped off at her workplace.

And then came the moment everything changed.

One night, after a long shift, Koketso told Sipho she was exhausted.
Not even ten minutes later, he was parked outside the store, leaning against his car with a takeaway bag in his hand.

"I couldn't let you go home hungry," he said softly.

It was such a small gesture, yet it hit her heart like thunder.

Tebogo had never done things like that — not because he didn't want to, but because he couldn't. His financial struggles limited him.

But deep inside, Koketso hated admitting that she liked how easy life felt with Sipho.

She liked the ease.
She liked the comfort.
She liked the speed.
She liked the attention.

Was it the money?
No, not the money itself.
It was what the money represented — progress, stability, certainty, the future she always wanted.

Sipho represented the life she dreamed of.
Tebogo represented the life she lived.

Slowly, guilt settled in her chest.
She found herself quieter around Tebogo.
Distracted.
Distant.
Easily irritated.

He felt her slipping, but he didn't know why.

"Koketso, are we okay?" he asked one evening while they were walking home after buying groceries with the little they had that week.

She forced a smile. "Yah, we're fine. I'm just tired."

But Tebogo wasn't convinced.

He tried harder.
He called more.
He visited more.
He held her hand more tightly when they walked.

And the sad part?
The harder he tried, the more guilty she felt — and the more she unconsciously pulled away.

It was agony for her.
She loved him.
She respected him.
But she was no longer in love the way she used to be.

Affection had turned into obligation.
Love had turned into habit.
Their dreams now felt far away… and she didn't know how to bridge the distance.

And then came the day that broke both their hearts.

Tebogo came to see her unexpectedly after her shift.
She had just come out of Sipho's car — he had dropped off lunch and a few things she mentioned needing earlier.

She didn't expect Tebogo to be standing there.

The look on his face...
Pain.
Confusion.
Fear.
Love.
All mixed into one.

"Koketso... who was that?"

He wasn't accusing. He was pleading.

Her throat tightened immediately. Her hands began to shake.

"It's... it's just someone I know," she whispered.

Tebogo stepped closer, eyes glossy. "Koketso... don't lie to me. Please. I can feel you slipping away. I just want to know what's going on."

And she broke.

Not loudly.
Not dramatically.
She simply exhaled, and tears fell.

She didn't have the courage to explain her heart — how it was confused, how it felt pulled, how she felt seen and admired in ways she didn't know she longed for.

She didn't know how to tell Tebogo that he had done nothing wrong — and yet she still wanted something different.

Tebogo cried.
He begged softly:
"Please don't leave me. We can fix whatever is wrong. Just talk to me."

But Koketso couldn't speak.
She just whispered:

"I'm sorry."

The silence after that felt like a funeral.

Tebogo wiped his face and nodded slowly, as if he had been sentenced.

"So that's it?"
His voice was barely above a whisper.

She nodded again, crying harder now, the guilt suffocating her.

"Okay," he said, breaking inside. "Okay… I won't force you."

He walked away before she could change her mind — or before he collapsed from heartbreak.

Koketso watched him leave, the sound of his quiet sobs echoing in her mind long after he disappeared.

That night, she didn't sleep.

She felt like she had buried something sacred.
But she told herself she had chosen her future.
She told herself she had chosen progress.
She told herself she had chosen a man who could build with her — or build her.

What she didn't realize was that she had also chosen to leave behind the world that once held her softly...
including the version of herself that once believed love alone was enough.

And slowly — step by step — Koketso walked deeper into Sipho's world.

A world that looked golden at first glance...
but gold can hide many things beneath its shine.

# Chapter 3: The Golden Beginning

In the weeks after her breakup with Tebogo, Koketso found herself floating between guilt and relief—two emotions that rarely sit comfortably together. She cried a few nights, replaying their last conversation... the look in his eyes... the quiet pain in his voice. But even as her heart ached, something in her felt pulled forward, almost guided, into a different life.

And Sipho... he was right there to catch her.

Not forcefully.
Not loudly.
Just present.
Consistent.
Soft in the right places, firm in others.

He didn't rush her, but he made himself available in a way that filled every empty space she didn't even realize had opened up.

He checked in more.
He took her out more.
He listened more.
He cared more.

He became her comfort, her distraction, her new beginning.

And in the beginning, everything Sipho did felt like luxury—not because it was expensive, but because it was easy.

Life with Tebogo took effort.
So much effort.
Even their love required stretching, sacrificing, waiting, adjusting, praying.

But with Sipho?
Life felt fast. Smooth. Ready-made.

He didn't just open doors for her—he opened futures.

One warm afternoon, he brought her to a rooftop restaurant she had seen only on social media. She sat across from him, taking in the skyline, the sunset bleeding gold into the city below them. She felt like she had stepped into somebody else's life.

"This is beautiful," she whispered.

Sipho smiled, not at the view—but at her reaction.
"You deserve beautiful things, Koketso."

It was the kind of sentence that lands deep in a woman's chest—quiet, affirming, almost healing. She had spent years stretching R20 here, budgeting there, postponing dreams, sharing burdens. To hear that she deserved beauty, comfort, and ease... it awakened something inside her.

Something she didn't know had been sleeping.

Sipho didn't spoil her recklessly; he spoiled her strategically.
Thoughtfully.
Intentionally.

If she mentioned she needed new shoes for work, he bought her two pairs.
If she talked about her long taxi rides, he told her, "I'll fetch you from now on."
If she said she was stressed, he showed up with food before she could finish the thought.

It all looked like love.
Felt like love.
Tasted like love.

And Koketso embraced it.

Slowly, Sipho's world began to replace hers.

Her old routines faded.
Her old worries quieted.
Her old dreams shifted shape.
Her old life dimmed behind her like a blurry memory.

Soon, she wasn't taking taxis.
She wasn't walking home from work.
She wasn't stressing over small expenses.
She wasn't carrying her life on her back anymore.

Sipho carried it for her.

And she didn't notice when that shift went from comforting to binding.

"Why don't you keep your money for yourself?" he told her one day as he paid for everything with ease. "You work too hard. Let me take care of you."

It sounded harmless.
It sounded loving.
And Koketso, tired from years of stretching coins, accepted it without thinking twice.

Before long, Sipho introduced her to his family.

They welcomed her warmly—especially because Sipho rarely brought women home. His mother hugged her tightly, studying her face as if she were reading her future.

"You're a good girl," she said softly. "I can tell."

His siblings greeted her like she was already part of the family.
Everyone treated her with a respect she wasn't used to.

It felt safe.
It felt promising.
It felt like she had finally arrived somewhere she always hoped to be.

Then one evening, Sipho held her hand and said the words that sealed her fate.

"Koketso… I want you to be my wife."

She froze—not from fear, but from disbelief.

Marriage?
Her?
This soon?

But Sipho had a way of making everything feel right—like every step he asked her to take was exactly where she was supposed to land.

"You're my peace," he said. "I don't want to lose you. Let's build something real."

He said it with a certainty that made it impossible to doubt him.

Koketso felt a flutter of joy rise through her chest, swallowing whatever little hesitation she had left.

She said yes.

It was a yes born from excitement.
A yes born from relief.
A yes born from the desire to rewrite her life.
A yes born from wanting love that was easier, brighter, faster.

A yes born from believing Sipho was her destiny.

Their marriage happened quickly—not rushed, just… efficient.
Sipho organized most of it.
He paid for everything without blinking.
He made every decision seem effortless.

People envied Koketso.
Her friends told her she was lucky.
Her mother cried tears of joy.

And Koketso?
She felt like she was stepping into the life she had always imagined.

After the wedding, Sipho suggested she move in with him.

There was no pressure—just convenience, practicality, and love woven together.

"Why should you struggle alone?" he asked with a gentle smile. "Let's live together as husband and wife."

She agreed.

His home was spacious, clean, orderly—nothing like the cramped rooms she was used to. She walked through the hallway, touching the furniture, the walls, the framed photos, marveling at how her life had transformed so quickly.

It felt too good to question.

But slowly, Sipho's protective nature began to shift shape—so subtly she didn't register it.

When she mentioned a long shift at work, he frowned.

"You don't need that stress anymore."

When she talked about saving for university again, he brushed her cheek and said:

"My love… you don't need to chase stress. I will provide. Focus on us."

When she tried to visit a friend, he said:

"Are you sure she's a good influence? Some friends don't want to see you happy."

When she got home late from work, he asked:

"Why must you suffer like this? I hate seeing you tired. Maybe it's time to think about leaving that job."

He didn't shout.
He didn't demand.
He didn't force.

He just suggested.

Gently.
Lovingly.
Convincingly.

And Koketso, lost in the glow of her new life, saw it as care.

As love.
As protection.
As leadership.

She didn't notice that with every suggestion, a small piece of her independence quietly slipped away.

For now, she was floating in the golden beginning —blinded by the shine, unaware that this glow was the first layer of a cage she would one day fight to escape.

# Chapter 4: Motherhood & Isolation

Tebogo never imagined his world could fall apart twice — first when Koketso walked away, and again when he saw her wedding pictures on Facebook.

He wasn't even looking for them. A friend sent them in a group chat:
"Isn't this your ex?"

And there she was.

Koketso.
In a white dress.
Glowing.
Smiling.
Standing next to a man who looked like he had everything Tebogo wished he could've given her.

His heart sank to the floor.
It felt unreal — like a nightmare someone else was having.
Just months ago, they were planning a future.

Saving together.
Dreaming together.
Struggling together.

Now she belonged to someone else.

He stared at the photos for a long time, scrolling slowly, each picture slicing deeper.
The comments didn't help:

"Beautiful couple!"
"Congratulations Mrs. Mokoena!"
"Your husband is such a good man."

It was as if the world had rewritten Koketso's memory — and erased him from her story entirely.

Tebogo tried to move on.
He dated.
He tried to laugh again.
He tried to forget.

But every woman he met felt temporary — like a placeholder.
Because the truth was simple and painful:
He still wanted Koketso.
He still loved Koketso.
And now she was someone else's wife.

The betrayal wasn't that she moved on.
It was how quickly she became someone new.

He didn't trust women anymore.
Not after that.
Not after losing the only one he had ever believed in.

While Tebogo was drowning in heartbreak, Koketso's life looked perfect from the outside.

Her body changed, softened, and glowed with pregnancy.
Her skin looked flawless — people kept telling her she was more beautiful than ever.
Her petite figure now carried new life, and she felt a strange mix of pride and fear.

Sipho was overjoyed.

He held her belly at night, whispering prayers and sweet promises.
He spoiled her even more.
He made her feel like royalty.

"Koketso," he'd say, brushing her cheek, "You're a queen. My queen. You shouldn't stress. Let me take care of everything."

And he did.

He bought all the groceries — she didn't even need to make a list. He knew exactly what was missing, exactly what she craved, exactly what needed restocking.
He made sure she never carried heavy bags.
He made sure she sat down when she cooked.
He made sure she slept whenever she felt tired.

At first, Koketso felt lucky — blessed even.

She told her friends:
"My husband is so good. He doesn't let me stress. He does everything for me."

What she didn't notice was the quiet shift happening beneath the sweetness.

Sipho gave her everything — except cash.

Not a single rand in her hand.
Not pocket money.
Not transport money.
Not emergency money.

"Just tell me what you need, my love," he'd say.
"I'll get it."

And because she trusted him, Koketso didn't think it was strange.

He wasn't refusing — he was managing.
He wasn't controlling — he was taking care of her.
He wasn't limiting her — he was protecting her.

At least, that's how she saw it.

After all, she loved him.
He treated her like a queen.
He made life easier.

But slowly, the ease became dependency.

If she wanted airtime, she had to ask.
If she needed a new bra, she had to ask.
If she wanted to visit her mother, she had to ask.
If she had cravings, she had to ask.

And Sipho's answers were always gentle, loving, calm:

"Of course, my love."
"No problem."
"You don't have to worry."
"I'll take care of it."

But every time she asked, she handed him a little more control — without realizing it.

Her dream of studying psychology felt further away now.
Whenever she mentioned school, Sipho pulled her close and kissed her forehead.

"You don't need to stress your mind," he whispered. "You're carrying my child. You need peace. School will always be there."

It sounded so loving.
So protective.
So convincing.

And Koketso believed him.

She stopped researching universities.
She stopped saving.
She stopped imagining lecture halls and textbooks and late-night studying.

Pregnancy became her world.
Sipho became her world.

Meanwhile, the cracks of isolation were forming quietly around her.

She visited her friends less — pregnancy tired her out, she told herself.
She called her mother less — Sipho always wanted her to rest.
She spent more time indoors — he preferred her safe at home.
She stopped going anywhere without him driving her — he said it was dangerous for her to walk or take taxis now.

She didn't see it as isolation.
She saw it as love.

As care.
As family building.
As stability.

Only later would she understand the truth:

That sometimes the softest cages are built from the sweetest gestures.

And sometimes the most dangerous control is the kind that feels like protection.

For now, Koketso was glowing.
Pregnant.
Loved.

Comfortable.
Cared for.

And Sipho?

He was building a world where she needed him for everything — slowly, methodically, lovingly.

She didn't know it yet…
but this was the beginning of the deepest loneliness she would ever experience —
a loneliness wrapped in love, hidden behind comfort, disguised as security.

A golden cage is still a cage.
It just shines too beautifully for the prisoner to notice.

# Chapter 5: The Critic Emerges

Birth changes something in a woman.
Not just her body — her eyes, her heart, her awareness.

When Koketso gave birth, she felt both powerful and fragile at the same time. The moment she held her baby, she felt something awaken deep inside her — something Sipho couldn't touch, couldn't control, couldn't dim.

Motherhood opened her eyes.

Sipho was attentive in the beginning — taking pictures, showing the baby off, buying small gifts, praising her for being "such a strong woman." He held the baby with pride, told every visitor how lucky he was to have Koketso, how beautiful she looked even after giving birth.

For a moment, she felt like her life had meaning beyond his world.

That feeling didn't last long.

Three months after giving birth, Koketso brought up school again, her old dream resurfacing now that the baby was settling into a routine.

"Babe," she said carefully, while folding baby clothes, "do you remember I told you I wanted to apply to university again?"

Sipho didn't even look up from his phone.

"Hmmm? Oh… school."
He paused only a second.
"You're not ready, my love. The baby is still small. You need rest. Stress is not good for you."

She felt the disappointment drop into her stomach like a stone.

"But I can manage—" she tried to explain.

Sipho finally looked at her.

"Koketso. Listen to me."
His tone was calm, but firm.
"You don't need to rush. I provide. Everything you need is here. Why must you go struggle with books when you have a baby to raise?"

It sounded logical.
Reasonable.
Protective.

But something in his tone left no room for her opinion.

She let it go — for that day.

Weeks passed, and Koketso began to notice things she once ignored.

Sipho went wherever he wanted — out with friends, to his siblings' houses, business errands, short trips — without asking, without discussing, without considering her.

But Koketso?
She couldn't even go buy bread without informing him.

Not because he shouted.
Not because he forbade her.
But because every time she tried to leave, he reminded her:

"It's dangerous. I'll go."
"You're tired. Rest."

"You don't need to walk in the sun."
"Just tell me what you want."

And because he framed everything as care, she felt guilty for even wanting to step outside.

But the danger wasn't outside.

The danger was how small her world had become.

Sipho bought everything — the groceries, the baby's items, the cleaning products — all without asking her what she wanted or needed.
If she mentioned something, he'd dismiss it:

"I know what the house needs."
"Don't stress yourself."
"I already bought everything necessary."

The more he "handled" things, the more invisible she became.

Koketso realized one quiet morning, while sitting on the edge of their bed, breastfeeding, that she didn't have a single coin to her name.

Not one rand.

Every single thing she needed — food, pads, lotion, airtime — she had to ask for.

Every request made her feel smaller.
Made her feel like a child.
Made her feel like she didn't own her life anymore.

She began to ask less, choosing to go without rather than hear him say:

"Okay, I'll get it."

He made it sound like love.
But her spirit felt the difference.

One evening she tried, very gently, to talk about it.

"Sipho… I don't like having to ask for everything."

He laughed softly, brushing her cheek.
"You're my wife. What must you need money for? Just tell me when you want something and I'll provide."

"But… it would help if I could have my own small money, you know? Just… something for myself."

Sipho's smile faded.

"Koketso, don't start this. You know I take care of you. Why must you handle money when I'm here?"

The room went quiet.

Something cold settled in her stomach.

That night, she cried silently, facing the wall — careful not to wake the baby, careful not to let Sipho hear the inner breaking he was causing without lifting a hand or raising his voice.

Months went by like this, and Koketso felt more trapped than loved.

And then…
she missed her period.

Again.

When she told Sipho she might be pregnant, his face lit up with pride.

"Oh thank God," he said, hugging her. "Another blessing. Another baby. My queen is giving me another child!"

Koketso forced a smile.

Inside, she was sinking.

She loved her baby.
She wanted to be a mother.
But another pregnancy meant:

- no school
- no independence
- no small job
- no freedom
- no personal money
- more isolation
- more control
- more asking for everything

And Sipho confirmed her fears instantly.

"Don't even think about school," he said. "Focus on the baby. Focus on being a mother. Stress is not for you. Leave the life and the plans to me. You just rest."

Those words crushed her.

Rest.

As if she were furniture.
As if she had no dreams.
As if motherhood replaced her identity.

He held her tightly, kissing her forehead.

"You don't need a job. You don't need school. You don't need money. I am your husband. I provide."

And for the first time, the sentence didn't feel romantic.

It felt like a door closing.

Koketso sat on the bed later that night, hands on her belly — this belly that carried life, joy, blessing — and she felt a tear fall.

Not from sadness.
Not from joy.
But from the piercing realization that her life was shrinking while Sipho's life expanded without limits.

He came and went freely.
He had money in his wallet, his phone, his bank account.
He made decisions.
He moved.
He lived.

But Koketso?

She was sinking deeper and deeper into a life where the walls were soft, warm, and protected — but still walls.

A life where she was safe, but not free.
Loved, but not heard.
Cared for, but not respected.

Sipho didn't raise his voice.
He didn't hit her.
He didn't insult her.

He simply removed her choices...
one sweet sentence at a time.

And now she was pregnant again —
carrying another baby in a world where she felt more invisible than ever.

This was the beginning of the heaviness she
would one day fight to escape —
a heaviness wrapped in comfort,
a heaviness disguised as love.

Because a cage built from gold is still a cage.
And Koketso had finally begun to see the bars.

# Chapter 6: The Weight of His Words

Giving birth the second time drained Koketso more than she expected.
Her body felt heavier, slower, tired in a way she could not explain.
Her days were filled with feeding, bathing, crying, sleepless nights, and holding two small children who needed her constantly.

There was no "mother glow" this time.
Just exhaustion.
Silent overwhelm.
And a loneliness she didn't dare say out loud.

She gained weight — gently at first, then noticeably.
Her stomach softened.
Her arms thickened.
Her face rounded.
Her clothes stopped fitting.

And Sipho noticed — not with concern, but with irritation.

One morning, while she was breastfeeding, he walked past her and said with a frown:

"Why are you looking so messy these days? You don't even try anymore."

The words pierced her.
She swallowed hard, pretending not to hear.

But Sipho didn't stop.

First, the small remarks:

"Maybe drink more water."
"You don't need to dish up twice at night."
"You know breastfeeding isn't a license to overeat."

Then the sharper ones:

"You're getting too big now."
"Is this how a young wife should look?"
"Koketso… honestly, you're embarrassing yourself."

Her confidence crumbled piece by piece.

One afternoon, she was eating a fatcake in the kitchen — a tiny comfort in a long, stressful day — when Sipho stopped, stared, and said:

"People who look like you shouldn't be eating fatcakes."

Her heart fell.
The fatcake felt like a stone in her hand.

And then came the comparisons.

"Look at Thembi. Four kids! Four! And you wouldn't even say it by looking at her.
But you? Two kids and I can't even lift you."

Each sentence sliced her deeper.

He said it casually, like it was normal.
Like her feelings didn't matter.
Like her body existed for his approval.

Soon, Sipho became ashamed to be seen with her.

When other couples invited them for gatherings, he always answered:

"No, we won't make it."
"Koketso is tired."
"We're staying in."

And in private, he said the words that finally broke her:

"I don't want people looking at you like this."

Restaurant dates disappeared.
If they went out at all, Koketso had to beg — beg for the chance to feel human, to dress up, to be outside.

Even during their children's birthday parties — events Sipho loved displaying — he humiliated her with "jokes" about her weight while guests laughed.

Everyone laughed.
Except Koketso.

Inside, she was collapsing.

Then Sipho bought her a car.

Not a gift.
Not freedom.
Not love.

A strategy.

At first she told herself:
"He wants me to have independence."

But slowly she understood the truth:

He didn't buy her a car so she could move freely.
He bought her a car so she wouldn't sit in his anymore.
So he could hide her.
So he wouldn't be seen with her.

And now that she no longer looked like the beautiful woman he once adored, suddenly he didn't care where she went.

"Go see your family if you want," he'd say. "I'm busy."

No more checking.
No more concern.
No more "stay home, my love, it's dangerous."

He simply didn't care.
She was no longer his trophy.

Meanwhile, her family and friends began noticing the cracks.

"You look tired, Koketso…"
"Take a walk, my girl."
"You need to get your life back."
"You're too young to be this drained."

Everyone could see she was fading —
everyone except Sipho.

Then came the day everything shattered more deeply.

One afternoon, she drove to the store —
messy bun, oversized t-shirt, leggings stretched tight, a spirit too tired to pretend —
and as she stepped out of her car, she looked up and froze.

Tebogo.

He had just parked two rows away.
He got out of his car — not fancy, not loud, but respectable.

He looked healthy.
Confident.
Peaceful.

He closed his door, walked around the car, and opened the passenger side.

A beautiful woman stepped out.
Slim.
Dress fitting perfectly.
Hair neat.
Face glowing.

Tebogo smiled at her — a soft, genuine smile Koketso knew better than anyone.

Her breath caught.
Her hands trembled.

Tebogo closed the door gently, laughed softly at something the woman said…
and when he lifted his head, their eyes met.

Koketso froze.

Shock.
Shame.
Embarrassment.
Regret.
All hit her like a wave.

Tebogo's expression changed instantly.
Surprise.
Recognition.
And something softer — concern?
Sadness?

He took one small step forward.
He opened his mouth, about to greet her.

"Koketso—?"

But before he could finish, before she could see anything more, before he could walk closer —

she turned around abruptly and rushed into the store, disappearing into the crowd.

Tebogo stood there for a moment...
confused...
concerned...
watching the spot where she vanished.

But she was gone.

Inside the store, Koketso leaned against a shelf, her chest tight, tears burning behind her eyes.

She hadn't just run from Tebogo.

She had run from the reflection of who she once was...
and the painful truth of who she had become.

# Chapter 7: Control & Dependence

The deeper Koketso sank into her new reality, the more Sipho rose into his.

With two children, her days blurred into one endless routine — waking up tired, cleaning, cooking, feeding, bathing, listening to cries, nursing stomach cramps, fighting headaches, packing away toys, washing bottles, folding tiny clothes, surviving.

Sipho hardly noticed the chaos.
He came home to a house cleaned, children fed, and dinner ready.

He never asked how her day was.
He never asked how she felt.
He never asked what she needed.

But if her hair wasn't neatly done?
If she skipped makeup?
If she wore an old t-shirt because she hadn't managed to wash her nicer clothes?

He noticed immediately.

"You're always looking untidy lately."
"You don't even try anymore."
"You're becoming lazy, Koketso."

Her self-esteem thinned like paper.

What Koketso didn't know was that Sipho's behaviour wasn't random…
he had been talking about her behind her back.

One afternoon, Sipho met his close friend Thabo for drinks.
They laughed at jokes, discussed business, talked about the kids — and then Sipho leaned in, lowering his voice as if speaking about a burden.

"Bruh, my wife has really changed."
He sighed dramatically.
"She's let herself go. She doesn't look like the girl I married."

Thabo frowned.
"Has she said she's struggling? Postpartum is real, you know. Two kids aren't easy."

Sipho shook his head dismissively.

"No, it's not that. She just... doesn't care anymore. I keep telling her to look after herself. I'm worried about her health."

He said it with such conviction that even he sounded convinced —
as if he actually cared about her health and not how her body made him look in public.

Thabo sipped his drink and looked at him carefully.

"Maybe she's depressed. Or bored. She's always home. Women need something to do too. Why don't you help her start a small business? Even an online thing. Or let her go back to school. She needs a life outside the house."

Sipho raised his eyebrows sharply, almost offended.

"A business? School? For what? She doesn't need all that."

Thabo looked confused.
"Why not? It would give her confidence. Purpose. It might even help her lose weight naturally. She can't just be home all day, every day. Anyone would gain weight like that."

Sipho leaned back in his chair, a slow smirk forming.

"I don't want a woman who works."

Thabo blinked.
"What? Why?"

"Women who work aren't submissive," Sipho said proudly.
"They start feeling themselves too much. They start thinking they're equal to you. I don't want that nonsense in my home."

Thabo was quiet now, studying Sipho with a seriousness that replaced all jokes.

"So you WANT her to depend on you?"

Sipho didn't hesitate.

"Yes. A woman must depend on her man. That's how you keep your home in order."

Thabo shook his head slightly.

"Sipho... be careful. You might think you're controlling the situation, but you're breaking her. A woman can't live like that forever."

Sipho waved him off.

"Please, man. Don't lecture me. I know my wife. If I give her too much freedom, she'll forget her place. She'll start disrespecting me. I must stay the man in my own house."

Thabo leaned forward, voice low.

"And what about how she feels? How she's shrinking? How she looks tired all the time? You can't build confidence by taking it away."

Sipho shrugged coldly.

"She'll be fine. She must just lose weight and look like a wife again."

Thabo stared at him for a long moment.

"You're not worried about her, Sipho. You're protecting your ego."

Sipho's jaw tightened.

"Think what you want."

What Sipho didn't realize was that narcissists always reveal themselves in private conversations —
and this one revealed everything:

His fear of empowered women.
His desire for control.
His pride in being needed.
His obsession with image.
His lack of empathy.
His belief that love should be earned through obedience.
His use of 'concern' as a weapon.

Meanwhile, back at home, Koketso felt her life shrinking even further.

Without money, she couldn't leave.
Without education, she couldn't grow.
Without support, she couldn't heal.
Without encouragement, she couldn't rise.

Every time she tried to voice a dream, Sipho shut it down:

"School? No."
"Work? No."
"A small business? Why? I provide."
"Confidence? For what? Just relax."

Her world was now Sipho's house.
Sipho's schedule.
Sipho's rules.
Sipho's money.
Sipho's control.

And whether he admitted it or not — he loved the new Koketso, the one with low confidence, soft voice, lowered eyes, and a shrinking identity.

She was easier to control.
Easier to silence.
Easier to keep.

He didn't just clip her wings.
He convinced her she didn't need them.

And that was the darkest form of control.

# Chapter 8: Cracks in the Throne

People often say that a man's home reflects his spirit.

Sipho didn't believe that.

He believed money was enough.
Control was enough.
Authority was enough.
Being "the man" was enough.

But what Sipho didn't understand — what he never imagined — was that you cannot keep winning when the person you wake up next to every day cries silently because of you.

A home cannot flourish when:

- one heart is breaking,
- one soul is shrinking,
- one person is dimming,
- and the other pretends not to notice.

Success grows where peace lives.
Sipho had money, but he did not have peace.

And slowly… quietly… his victories began to fade.

It started with small things.

Clients delayed payments.
Deals he was confident about suddenly stalled.
People he trusted began disappointing him.
He was constantly irritated, easily angered, snapping at everyone.

The aura in the house was heavy.

Koketso wasn't praying for him anymore.
She wasn't rooting for him.
She wasn't supporting him spiritually.

She couldn't.

Her spirit was too tired.
Too drained.
Too bruised.

Every morning she woke up with tears dried on her cheeks.
Sipho pretended not to notice, but the universe did.

A man cannot draw blessings from a woman whose heart he breaks daily.

Where there is no harmony, nothing grows.

Sipho thought he was still in control.
He thought he could keep winning on his own.
But the cracks started showing.

One afternoon, he received a call that made his stomach drop.

A major business deal collapsed — a deal he had bragged about for months.
Something about paperwork, a partner pulling out, "unforeseen complications."

He punched the steering wheel so hard his knuckles bled.

Another deal fell through a week later.
People started dodging his calls.
His usual luck was gone.

Nothing was working.

And every night he came home to the same sight:

Koketso in the kitchen, quiet.
Koketso folding laundry, distant.
Koketso breastfeeding, staring into space.
Koketso lying on her side, facing away from him.

She didn't fight.
She didn't shout.
She didn't complain.

But that silence carried more power than any argument.

He felt it.
But instead of apologizing, Sipho grew angrier.

"What's wrong with you now?" he snapped one night.

Koketso didn't answer.

"Must I beg you to be a wife?"

Still, she didn't answer.

Her silence frustrated him — but deep down, Sipho felt something he didn't want to name:

He felt the house slipping out of his spiritual control.

You cannot break your partner and expect the home to remain whole.

He wanted her spirit quiet — but not this quiet.
He wanted her submission — but not her emotional death.
He wanted her to obey — but not to disappear.

He wanted her body present but her spirit alive enough to serve his ego.

But you cannot choose which parts of a person die when you kill their confidence.

And Koketso's spirit was fading fast.

Sipho's business continued to shake.

Unexpected bills.
Lost contracts.
Bad decisions.
Clashing partnerships.
Financial strain.

He blamed everyone —
except the man in the mirror.

Meanwhile, Koketso began to feel something she hadn't felt in years:

An awakening.

It was small at first — a thought, a whisper, a tiny voice that said:

"You deserve more."

When Sipho looked at her with disgust…
when he insulted her body…
when he ignored her tears…
when he left her alone to drown in the chaos of motherhood…

something inside her snapped quietly.

She didn't scream.
She didn't fight.
She didn't threaten to leave.

But she started observing.
Seeing clearly.
Understanding deeply.

The man she married wanted control — not partnership.
He wanted a servant — not a wife.
He wanted to stay "the man" — by keeping her small.

And while Sipho was losing control of his business, Koketso slowly began to regain control of her mind.

For the first time in a long time…

she began to imagine a life outside the cage.

She didn't know how she would escape.
She didn't know when.
She didn't know what she would lose.

But she knew this:

A marriage cannot survive on one broken spirit.
A home cannot win when only one partner is allowed to breathe.
A man cannot prosper while suffocating the woman connected to his destiny.

Something was shifting.

In Koketso.
In Sipho.
In the atmosphere.

The throne Sipho built was cracking.

And soon...
it would collapse entirely.

# Chapter 9: Picking Up the Pieces

Life has a way of humbling even the strongest men — especially the ones who believe they are untouchable.

Sipho had built his identity on being "the provider."
The one everyone leaned on.
The one with solutions.
The one people praised.

His entire family depended on him —
his parents, his siblings, his cousins, even extended relatives who knew Sipho as the successful one.

So when life struck back, it hit every corner of his world.

His business didn't just struggle — it collapsed.

At first it was small things:
a client delaying payment,
a supplier refusing credit,
a simple deal falling apart.

Then it snowballed.
Fast.
Violent.
Unstoppable.

Sipho tried to hide it.

But the day he couldn't even buy bread for the children —
that was the day Koketso realized how deep the fall really was.

"Mama, I want bread," their youngest cried.

Sipho looked away.
Frustrated.
Ashamed.
Helpless.

Later that evening, Koketso approached him gently.

"Sipho… maybe I should go look for a job. Just to help until things get better."

He snapped instantly.

"No. This is temporary. I don't want you working. I don't want people thinking I can't provide. I'm still the man of this house."

His ego spoke louder than his reality.

But reality didn't care.

Bills piled up.
Electricity ran out.
Groceries finished faster than they could stretch them.
Their savings disappeared.
The landlord grew impatient.

Finally, they had to downsize — from a spacious home to a small apartment.
Two kids sharing one bedroom.
Koketso storing pots under the bed because the kitchen was too small.

Even then, Sipho still couldn't keep up.

One afternoon, Koketso said quietly:

"Let me ask my family for help, just for now—"

Sipho slammed his hand on the table.

"What do you want them to think of me? That I can't provide for my own family? Do you want to humiliate me?!"

She stepped back, startled.

"It's not humiliation, Sipho... it's help."

He shook his head aggressively.

"No! I will never let your family say I failed."

She tried the other option.

"Then ask your friends..."

"So they can laugh at me?" he shouted. "You act like you never struggled before! Why can't you handle a little hardship?"

Koketso looked around the small, empty apartment.

A "little hardship" was an understatement.

Days passed.
Nights passed.
Nothing improved.

Until one morning, Koketso woke up hungry — and watched her children cry because there was no food.

Something inside her snapped.

She walked to the kitchen, opened the cupboards, and saw only flour left — flour Sipho had once bought in bulk when times were good.

She checked her bank app.
There was a small amount she forgot about — maybe money refunded from an old data purchase, maybe leftover change.
It didn't matter.
It was enough for something.

She dried her tears, grabbed her bag, and walked out.

Sipho's voice cracked behind her:

"Where are you going? Hey! Koketso! I'm talking to you!"

She didn't flinch.

She didn't look back.

She simply said:

"Well, someone has to make sure the kids eat."

He fell silent — embarrassed, angry, exposed.

Without money, the power he once used to control her had evaporated.

Koketso drove to the store and bought butter, sugar, eggs — just enough to bake.

When she came home, Sipho was in the living room, pretending to scroll on his phone, pretending not to notice his own helplessness.

She went straight to the kitchen, opened her old baking recipe book — the one she hadn't touched in years — and began mixing ingredients.

The smell of fresh biscuits filled the house.

She gave some to the children first.
They smiled for the first time in days.

Sipho hovered, confused and ashamed.

She kept baking.

The next morning, she packed the biscuits into a bucket, got dressed, and headed to the door.

Sipho's voice followed her, tense and irritated:

"Where are you going? What's in that bucket? Koketso, answer me!"

She turned around slowly, her voice steady and tired of his excuses.

"I'm going to try and sell these biscuits," she said firmly.
"I cannot sit by and watch my kids starve just because you don't want me to work… or do you have a better plan?"

Sipho opened his mouth, but nothing came out.
He had no plan.
No money.
No solution.

All he had left was pride —
and pride couldn't feed children.

She didn't wait for him to respond.

She walked out.

At the corner near the taxi rank, she sat with her bucket of biscuits.

At first, people walked past.

She felt nervous, exposed, unsure of herself.

Then someone bought one.
Then another person stopped.
Then someone asked:

"Sister, these smell amazing — do you have more?"

By afternoon, word had spread that a new woman was selling nice biscuits at the corner.

Taxi drivers.
Shoppers.
School kids.
Mothers walking home.

One by one, they bought from her.

Within hours, she sold out.

She stood there, staring at the empty bucket, shocked...
and proud.

She bought more ingredients.
Went home.
Baked again.

The next day — she sold out again.

For the first time in a long time...
Koketso felt something awaken inside her:

Independence.
Confidence.
Pride.
Hope.

Each biscuit she sold was a piece of her life returning.

Each rand she earned was a chain breaking.

And Sipho?

He watched her —
confused, threatened, insecure —
realizing the woman he had controlled for years was rising again.

Her confidence was returning.

And he didn't know how to stop it.

Because this time…

he had no money,
no power,
no excuses,
and no control.

This time…

Koketso was reclaiming her life.

# Chapter 10: Finding Her Voice

Sipho didn't know what to do with this new version of Koketso.

The Koketso who left the house with purpose.
The Koketso who came home with money SHE earned.
The Koketso who no longer asked him for anything.
The Koketso who didn't tremble when he raised his voice.

Her confidence wasn't loud — it was steady.
And that steady confidence terrified Sipho more than any argument ever could.

He tried to pretend nothing had changed.

"So now you're a businesswoman?" he said one evening with a mocking smile as she walked in, smelling of butter and vanilla.

She didn't respond.

He tried again the next day.

"So this is your life now? Sitting at a street corner selling biscuits?"

She wiped the counter calmly.

"It's honest work," she said. "And it feeds the kids."

Her calmness frustrated him more than anger would have.

He wanted her small.
He wanted her unsure.
He wanted her dependent.

But now?
She wasn't any of those things.

The more she rose, the more Sipho's insecurity grew — until one night, he finally exploded.

"You think you're a big woman now because you're selling biscuits?" he shouted.
"You think this nonsense makes you better? You're embarrassing me!"

Koketso looked up from the table slowly.

For the first time in years...
her eyes didn't drop.
Her shoulders didn't shrink.
Her voice didn't shake.

She stood up.
Not rushed.
Not dramatic.

Just steady.
Certain.
Unmoved.

"Sipho," she said, her voice calm but razor sharp, "respect me."

He blinked, stunned.

She continued.

"I have carried your children.
I have sacrificed my dreams.
I have been quiet when you insulted me.
I have swallowed pain you don't even know exists.
But I will NOT be disrespected anymore."

Sipho opened his mouth, but Koketso lifted her hand slightly.

"I'm talking. You will listen."

Sipho froze.

She had never spoken to him like this.

Koketso took a deep breath, her heart steady — not because she wasn't scared, but because she finally knew her worth.

"I am doing what YOU failed to do," she said.
"I'm feeding your children.
I'm keeping this house alive.
I'm the one making sure we don't sleep hungry.
So no — you will not belittle me ever again."

Sipho clenched his jaw, embarrassed, angry, exposed.

"You think I'm scared of you now?" he snapped.

"No," she said softly. "I think you're scared of losing control."

He stiffened.

Koketso stepped closer — not in aggression, but with an honesty that felt heavy, final.

"If you speak to me like that again," she whispered,
"if you insult me again,
if you try to break my spirit again…"

She paused.

"I will leave."

Sipho's eyes widened.

Koketso didn't shout.
She didn't throw things.
She didn't cry.

She simply meant it.

"And if I leave," she continued,
"I won't come back.
Not for you.
Not for this house.
Not for anything."

Sipho swallowed hard.

"You… you're threatening me?" he muttered.

"No," she said. "I'm telling you the truth."

The room was silent.

Sipho had never looked so small.
So shaken.
So disarmed.

For years, his power came from her silence.

But now?

She had a voice.
A purpose.
A source of income.
Confidence.
A life forming outside of him.

And nothing is more terrifying to a controlling man
than a woman who finally knows her power.

Koketso walked past him, picked up her recipe book, and set it on the kitchen table.

Her voice softened, but remained firm:

"I am rebuilding myself, Sipho. With or without your support."

Sipho stared at her —
the woman he broke trying to stand again
and realizing he could no longer stop her.

Because the day a woman finds her voice
is the day a controlling man loses his power.

# Chapter 11: Rebuilding on Equality

Sipho didn't change overnight —
but the day Koketso stood up to him, something inside him cracked.

Not his pride.
His denial.

For the first time in years, he saw himself clearly.

Saw the damage he caused.
Saw the weight she carried.
Saw the woman he once loved disappearing because of him.

And that night… he couldn't sleep.

The next morning, Koketso woke up before sunrise, ready to bake —
but when she walked into the kitchen, she froze.

The counters were clean.
The floor was swept.
The kettle was already boiled.

And Sipho...
Sipho was standing by the stove flipping eggs.

"Good morning," he said softly, almost shyly.

She stared.

Sipho had spoiled her with gifts and attention before — yes —
but he had NEVER woken up early to cook for her.
Never cleaned.
Never took care of the kids.
This was new.

"I made breakfast. Come eat before you start baking."

Koketso blinked.
Twice.

"What's going on?" she asked cautiously.

Sipho shrugged awkwardly.
"I just... want to help. Sit down. Eat."

She sat slowly, still watching him like she was waiting for the prank reveal.

He plated the food neatly, even added a piece of toast with margarine spread evenly corner to corner.
He placed it in front of her gently.

"You feed everyone," he said quietly. "Let me feed you today."

Her throat tightened.

She ate silently, still confused.

After breakfast, she tied her apron and prepared to start baking — but Sipho walked toward the bathroom.

"I'll bathe the kids today," he said. "And I'll take them to school."

Koketso stood there speechless, holding a bowl of flour.

"Sipho… are you sure?"

He nodded without turning back, because if he did, she might see the guilt in his eyes.

"I should have been helping a long time ago," he murmured.

She didn't reply.
She didn't trust her voice.

That day, while she was selling biscuits, Sipho arrived unexpectedly with a takeaway container.

"I brought you lunch," he said, smiling gently. "You always feed us. Let me feed you too."

Koketso looked around, embarrassed but also touched.
"Why are you doing all this?"

He swallowed.

"Because I saw you. Really saw you. And I didn't like the man I've been."

She didn't answer — but her silence wasn't rejection.
It was shock.

Before leaving, he asked softly:

"And these biscuits... they're really good. You have a skill, Koketso. A real one."

Her chest warmed.

Compliments from Sipho used to be rare.
Now they felt like rain after a long drought.

For days, Sipho continued:

- ✓ cleaning the house
- ✓ waking up early
- ✓ bathing the kids
- ✓ helping with homework
- ✓ dropping them at school
- ✓ calling to ask if she was okay
- ✓ bringing her lunch
- ✓ helping pack biscuits for the next day

And every single time, Koketso wondered:

Who is this man?
Where did the Sipho she knows go?
And why does this feel so new... and so painful?

One evening, she came home tired, smelling of butter and sugar — and found the dining table set beautifully.

Candles.
A simple meal.
Two plates.
A quiet atmosphere.

Sipho pulled out a chair for her.

"I thought we could talk," he said softly.

She sat slowly.

He took a deep breath.

"Koketso… I am sorry."

Real sorrow.
Not prideful.
Not rushed.
Not defensive.

"I said things I should never have said.
I controlled you.
I broke you.

I treated you like you were nothing without me.
And I was wrong."

Koketso's eyes filled with tears.

"I saw you becoming smaller every day," he continued.
"And I told myself it was your fault, not mine.
You gave me everything, and I gave you pain."

She wiped her cheek quietly.

"I don't deserve forgiveness," Sipho whispered.
"But I want to try. If you'll let me."

Koketso took a deep breath — strong, steady, sure.

"I need things to change," she said.
"I won't be silent again.
I won't shrink for anyone.
If we continue… it must be as equals."

Sipho nodded quickly.
"Yes. Anything you want."

"And I want to go to university," she added softly but firmly.

Sipho looked up, surprised.
"You… you still want to study?"

"Yes," she said confidently.
"I had dreams before life happened.
I wanted a degree. I wanted a career.
I paused my life for this family, but I won't pause anymore.
It's my turn now."

Sipho swallowed hard, guilt and admiration mixing in his eyes.

"I can't help financially," he said quietly, ashamed.
"But I'll support you in every other way.
Emotionally.
Practically.
With the house.
With the kids.
Whatever you need.
I'll make sure you have time to study."

Koketso nodded, her chest warming.

"That's all I needed," she said.
"Support. Respect. Partnership."

Sipho nodded again, humbled.

"You'll have it."

Koketso reached into her bag, pulled out an envelope, and slid it across the table.

"This is for your business," she said softly.
"Start it again. Properly.
You helped me once. Let me help you now."

Sipho stared at the envelope, stunned.

"I... I don't deserve this from you," he said, voice cracking.

Koketso looked at him gently but firmly.

"It's not about deserving.
It's about rebuilding.
Together."

Sipho lowered his head, overwhelmed.

"Thank you," he whispered.
"I won't waste this.
Or you."

For the first time in years, they sat together without tension.

No shouting.
No belittling.
No fear.
Just two imperfect people choosing to try again.

Because love doesn't survive on perfection —
it survives on effort.

And this time...

they were finally working as partners.
Not enemies.
Not strangers.
Not boss and servant.

Just Sipho.
And Koketso.
Rebuilding on equality.

# EPILOGUE — HER NEW BEGINNING

Two years later, Koketso stood on the campus grounds of the university she had once only dreamed about.
Her backpack felt heavy, but her heart felt light — freer than it had felt in over a decade.

She was no longer the girl who whispered her dreams.
She was the woman who walked toward them.

Her biscuit business had grown beyond the corner of the taxi rank.
She now had a small stall — painted pastel yellow, with her name proudly displayed.
People lined up for her biscuits.
Mothers, taxi drivers, schoolchildren.
Everyone called her:

"The Biscuit Queen."

But even sweeter than the biscuits was the way her life had changed.

The laughter in her home was different now.
Her children were happier, louder, more confident.
They ran to her after school shouting:

"Mama baked again!"
"Mama's famous!"
"Mama, can we help?"

And Sipho...
Sipho had changed too.

Not into a perfect man — those don't exist.
But into a present one.

He woke up early with her every morning.
He packed lunch for the kids.
He attended school meetings.
He helped with homework.
He kept the house running when her classes ran late.
He encouraged her when exams stressed her.
He told her:

"You're not alone anymore. We're building this life together."

His business slowly began to recover — not
because Koketso pushed him,
but because he finally pushed himself.

Respect had returned to their marriage.
Not fear.
Not control.
Not silence.

Respect.

One evening, after a long day of classes and baking, Koketso sat on the couch with a cup of tea.
The house was quiet except for the sound of her children giggling in their room.

Sipho sat beside her and placed a gentle hand on her thigh.

"You look tired," he said softly.
"Tired but fulfilled."

Koketso smiled.

"I am," she whispered.

Sipho took a deep breath — the kind that comes from a man who knows the value of what he almost lost.

"Thank you for giving us a second chance," he said.

Koketso turned to him with a small smile.

"Thank you," she replied, "for becoming a man who deserved it."

They didn't promise perfection.
They promised effort.
Growth.
Teamwork.

And sometimes…
that's more sacred than a fairy tale.

Because their story was no longer about who hurt who —
it was about who chose to change.

Who chose to grow.

And who chose to love again,
properly this time.

Koketso looked around her home — smaller than the old one, but fuller somehow.
Full of peace.
Full of humility.
Full of second chances.

She didn't rise alone.
She didn't rise for revenge.

She rose for herself.
For her children.
For the woman she was always meant to be.

And Sipho rose too —
not as her master,
but as her partner.

Together, imperfect but willing,
they built a new beginning.

A beginning rooted in respect,
not fear.

In teamwork,
not control.

In love that had learned how to behave.

And this time...
they both knew:

The real gold was never the lifestyle.
It was the growth.
The humility.
And the healing they chose.
Together.

# ABOUT THE AUTHOR

Thuli Marutle Leigh is a South African-born author and International ESL Teacher whose work blends emotional depth with meaningful life lessons. Her storytelling spans both children's literature and adult fiction, capturing the realities, challenges, and triumphs of everyday people with honesty and clarity.

Known for her powerful narratives and relatable characters, Thuli writes with the intention to inspire reflection, healing, and personal growth. Her books resonate with readers across cultures, offering hope, strength, and a reminder that second chances — in love, in life, and in self-worth — are always possible.

She currently lives and teaches abroad while continuing to build a growing library of impactful, transformative stories for global readers.

Koketso's love story begins with charm, stability, and the promise of a brighter future.

But as the years pass, her marriage shifts from affection to criticism, from protection to quiet control. Once confident and full of dreams, she finds herself shrinking inside a life that no longer resembles the one she imagined.

When Sipho's success collapses and their home is shaken to its core, Koketso discovers a strength she never knew she had. Through courage, hard work, and a renewed sense of identity, she begins to rebuild her life — and confront the parts of herself she lost along the way.

As she rises, Sipho is forced to face his own failures and choose between pride or transformation. Together, they must learn what partnership truly means: honesty, respect, humility, and shared responsibility.

A heartfelt and realistic story about identity, motherhood, emotional healing, and the power of trying again.

This is not a tale of escape — but a journey toward rebuilding love on equal ground.

www.ingramcontent.com/pod-product-compliance
Lightning Source LLC
Chambersburg PA
CBHW020359170426
43200CB00005B/225